T0207871

# TRIQUETRA

A COLLECTION OF POEMS INSPIRED BY:
THE MAIDEN THE MOTHER
THE WISE WOMAN

## CECILIA BRYDEN LAING
## PATRICIA RAY

**BALBOA.**PRESS
A DIVISION OF HAY HOUSE

Balboa Press books may be ordered through booksellers or by contacting:

Balboa Press
A Division of Hay House
1663 Liberty Drive
Bloomington, IN 47403
www.balboapress.com
1 (877) 407-4847

Because of the dynamic nature of the Internet, any web addresses or links contained in this book may have changed since publication and may no longer be valid. The views expressed in this work are solely those of the author and do not necessarily reflect the views of the publisher, and the publisher hereby disclaims any responsibility for them.

The author of this book does not dispense medical advice or prescribe the use of any technique as a form of treatment for physical, emotional, or medical problems without the advice of a physician, either directly or indirectly. The intent of the author is only to offer information of a general nature to help you in your quest for emotional and spiritual well-being. In the event you use any of the information in this book for yourself, which is your constitutional right, the author and the publisher assume no responsibility for your actions.

Any people depicted in stock imagery provided by Getty Images are models, and such images are being used for illustrative purposes only. Certain stock imagery © Getty Images.

Print information available on the last page.

ISBN: 978-1-9822-3692-2 (sc)
ISBN: 978-1-9822-3693-9 (e)

Balboa Press rev. date: 10/15/2019

# Dedication

This collection is a gift.

To my Mother;
For her words have been silent for far too long.

To my Grandmother;
For her ever-loving support and leadership.

To you, the Reader;
Enjoy! May these words whisper to you and resonate
with your soul; as they have whispered to us...
The Maiden
The Mother
The Wise Woman

With Love & Gratitude
Patricia Ray

# The Maiden

Child of the Country.................................................................1
Bras D'or Lament................................................................. 3
Empty City ......................................................................... 5
Dreams................................................................................ 7
Spring Dawn.........................................................................9
Irish Magic .........................................................................11

# The Mother

Wish for the Future................................................14
L-O-V-E.............................................................17
Cape Breton Wife..................................................19
The Song of the Woodsman........................................21
Winter Morning....................................................23
Lord, I am Afraid.................................................25
Tension............................................................26
Sanctuary..........................................................27
See These Things..................................................29
Respite............................................................31

# The Wise Woman

Life's Little Wonders............................................................35

Sailor Island ....................................................................36

Memories of Home ..............................................................39

Seasons............................................................................41

# Epilogue: The Ancestor and The Descendant

The Cane .................................................................... 44

Turtle Steps .............................................................. 47

AWAY...HOME? ........................................................ 48

Lifetime of Leaves ...................................................... 51

# The
# Maiden

# child of the Country

Shining dew in the morning sun
Dancing pearls as the day's begun
Soft brown earth between my toes
Barefoot and free as summer grows
Praising the evening as sunlight dims
Child of the country in daylight zone
Alive in the mountains and lakes of home.

CeCe

# Bras D'or Lament

The waters of Bras D'or
Beckon me home.
I see her shining blue waters
Wherever I roam.
Cool and inviting,
Softly kissing the sands;
Of the beaches we wandered
Dear love, hand in hand.
Away and away,
You've gone from me now;
Only god knows the reason
But I yet ask him, how
Could he see to deprive me
Of your sweet loving smile?
At least not forever;
No, not even a while.
Yes, time soothes the pain,
Only as mist on the hills
Lightens and fades,
But, what remains
Still is enough of a memory,
Wherever I roam;
For the waters of Bras D'or
To beckon me home.

CeCe

# Empty City

I was a child lost
Upon a crowded street
In a city of empty people
Passing by as in a dream
I called them brother
Called them sister
Yet they remained cold and mean

I passed them as the buildings
Left the faces made of stone
Felt the terror indescribable
Of the city night alone
The essence of human suffering
Screaming in the night
Wandered finally to the limits
Where the country comes in sight

Back to Mother Nature
To fields and mountains bold
Surrounded by innocence and beauty
And a shining love untold

CeCe

# Dreams

How I long for the simple life
Quiet nights and work filled days
Wide open spaces
Special places
Soft glow of firelight,
The lake in the moonlight;
Shining kitchen, neat yard;
Smell of home baked bread,
Fresh garden vegetables;
Wild blueberries and sky.
Patchwork quilts sewn together
On winter days of cold and snow.
While the t.v. shows the lives
Of people, I'll never have to know
Prayers of thanks to God
To be alive
When the sun rises over the hills
Spring showing its face
In the gold of daffodils
And the sweet smell of apple blossoms
Floats in the breeze.

CeCe

# Spring Dawn

As the sun rises over the mountains
In my dreams
You'll be with me again

Hand in hand
We will walk through the forest
And I'll know your sweet love again

Away, far away
I must journey
For my world holds no place
For a dream

But my heart will always be with you
On the hilltop close by the stream

Oh my love how it pains me to leave you
Yet we both know its all we can do
Til one day when these trials are over
When I'll be free to come home to you

CeCe

# Irish Magic

Here is a story
With a magical theme
Of two lovers meeting
In a St. Patrick's Day dream

Green was the gown
This good fairy wore
Green as the grass
On Ireland's fair shore

The prince he was dressed
In a scarlet cloak
Blood red it flowed
Over his white stallion's coat

She stood in the courtyard
Awaiting the sight
Of her lover who would
Carry her off through the night

He whisked her up on the stallion
And off and away
To his castle of stone
Until the breaking of day

When the magic was ended
With the coming of light
The lovers had vanished
From the mere mortal's sight.

CeCe

# The Mother

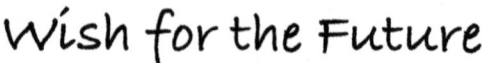

# Wish for the Future

As I watch you lying there my child
I wonder what the future holds
For you in years to come.

How can you maintain your loving ways
Yet gain the independence the world demands

How can we teach you of love?
How you have first to give so much of yours
Yet have enough self-respect
To realize when you can give no more

How in this upside down world
There is still beauty –
And that we must not forget
He who created it,

How to realize both the benefit of true education
Yet the satisfaction of physical labour,

May you learn to appreciate
The value of science
Both the good it can do
And the disaster it can bring.

May you be reasonably wealthy
In the riches of the world
But only after you have found riches of spirit

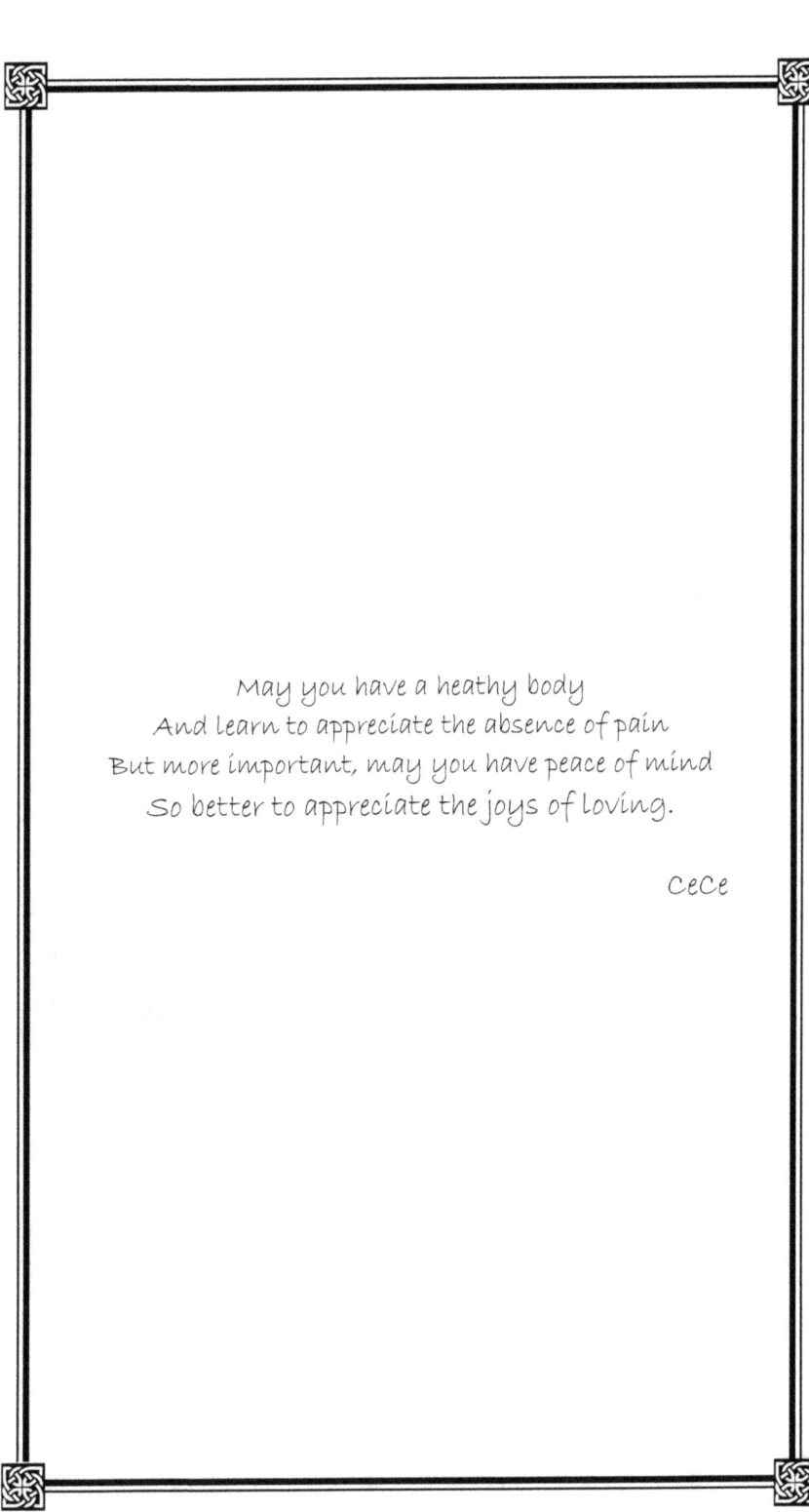

May you have a heathy body
And learn to appreciate the absence of pain
But more important, may you have peace of mind
So better to appreciate the joys of loving.

CeCe

# L-O-V-E

L – is for letting someone be themselves
without condemnation or criticism
O – is for only –
Only when we share is love possible
V – is for very –
Very important to communicate feelings
E – is for enough –
Enough respect for the other person

CeCe

# Cape Breton Wife

I've learned to make my own bread
Even picked the berries for the spread
Tried to save in summer's heat
For the winter we'd have to meet
Knowing that I've always found
Us poor as church mice
When spring comes round
I've prayed for work
For my man to do
Knowing there were no jobs to go to
I guess I'll be poor all of my life
I am a Cape Breton Wife.

CeCe

# The Song of the Woodsman

Rows of wood in neat little piles
All in a row up the mountain side
A road in the middle, brush over there
Cut it down before the budworm
Takes his share
With a Stihl, and a partner, and a pioneer too
The hours that you work are up to you.

CeCe

# Winter Morning

The rosy glow of dawn
Casts a blush on the winter ice
The high polish of a recent thaw
Reflects the growing brightness
In the east.
Crack, Crack –
The only sound in the February morn
The frost
Has the only voice that speaks

CeCe

# Lord, I am Afraid

Man has become a monster unguarded
The beauty of his mind somehow retarded
What has become of your image in him
Lord, I am afraid.

The beauty of sky, earth, sea and sun
Has been dirtied and clouded
By smoke, oil and scum.
To your lovely creation, what has been done?
Lord, I am afraid.

The memory of Calvary somehow has faded
They've forgotten your life
And the reason you gave it
Lord, I am afraid.

Has this world come to the end of its days?
Lord, I am afraid.

CeCe

# Tension

Worries and wishes cloud my mind
The work of yesterday falls behind
I sit here and ponder my plight
Trembling inside my nerves are so tight
My wants and my needs don't coincide
Physically inert
My mind's on a ride.

CeCe

# Sanctuary

When the world crowds around me
I long for peace again
To wander in the wilderness
To rest in a quiet glen
For the forest is understanding
Each tree a silent friend
No pity or malice given
Only sanctuary
On which to depend.

CeCe

# See These Things

Take a look for me
At the blue skies,
At the sun, sparkling
Like diamonds on the bay.

Take it all in,
And hold it for me.
For I am starving in my heart
For the sight,

My mind is tired
And my eyes are weary;
Of seeing people, and man-made things
Of the city.

My ears ache from the sound
Of a hundred voices.
How I wish they were the voices
Of the birds in the trees.

Look at these things, and think of me
Listen for my thank you
In the whisper of the breeze.

CeCe

# Respite

Take my hand and lead me
On the pathways of your dreams
Make my thoughts as one with yours
No barriers between.
Let us sit before the firelight
With silence as our friend
No worries for the moment
Or things with which we must contend
Give me but a day or two
Our lives with which to share
Let us make some memories
Joys to help us by the cares.

CeCe

# The
# Wise
# Woman

# Life's Little Wonders

The tears they come unbidden
Welling from my eyes
When I am held witness
To beauty in our lives.

To see the dawn of understanding
Fill the eyes of a friend
To know you've found a person
On whom you can depend.

To close the door to hatred
Let forgiveness rule supreme
Being able to accept troubled times
In the promise of a dream.

To touch the splendor of a rose
Uncurling from its bud
To cherish thoughts and memories
Of the people that you love.

CeCe

# Sailor Island

Our canon men are ready
Her fortress gates shut tight
Her fog shrouded battlements
Are ghostly in the light.

A ship lies weighing anchor
Lifting with the tide
She sails to France this morning
With our blessings she will ride

Many fortunes worth of treasures
Lay securely in her hold
We must save them from the enemy
Those Englishmen so bold

A sailor bids his family
And loving wife adieu
Eager in the prospect
Of seeing the home he knew

The captain gives his blessing
To the men upon the deck
God save us from disaster
From the horrors of a wreck

A cheer goes up from shore
As the ship sails out to sea
With these men all the treasures
And the people's trust will be

For the glory of his country
A man will often die
Yet there's a stronger force within
When greed is in his eye

A fever steals upon the minds
Of those in care of gold
His hand came out to claim this ship
With fortunes in her hold.

Sailing in strange waters
This ship was later seen
Searching to find a hark over
Where no man has ever been

As morning broke upon the water
A wonder to behold
A green and shadowed island
In a deep and peaceful cove.

Its shores so gently sloping
Rise straight out from the sea
So close, the men upon the ship
Can moor her to the trees.

Soon now all the treasures
Of a people and a land
Are carried to the island
And buried beneath the sand.

One man is left to guard the place
Until his friends return
For this duty he is told
A reward he will earn

For many years he walked the shore
Of this island now his home
What had happened to his friends
He had never known.

A battle was fought – upon the sea
The English: they had won
All hands were lost –
None were left to tell
What they had done.

CeCe

# Memories of Home

It seems so strange
That when you're grown
Some things never seem the same
As they did when you were home
When you came in from school
Didn't turn out the way it should
Even though you followed all mom's rules
Somehow there never seemed to be
Out of all the ones you bought
A single fish to taste the same
As the ones that dad caught
For those of us who've left it
Home, like us, has changed
Yet these simple memories we know
Will always be the same.

CeCe

# Seasons

The sun shines so bright,
The cool fall air is welcome,

Fresh and full
The season nears completeness

Growing plants showing
Their last blooms of summer,

If life is nature,
And nature is life;
Why isn't life as constant
As the seasons?

Only four changes per year,
If you please.

Yet, summer doesn't end overnight;
Even fall days have the hint of summer,

Even in the autumn years of this life
I feel the summer within.

The spirit of my life is ageless;
Only the body is lined and layered
Like time circles on a tree.

CeCe

41

# Epilogue:
# the Ancestor
# &
# the Descendant

# The Cane

A young country man was setting out on a two-day journey into town for supplies. His neighbor was an old maid and asked him if he would please keep an eye out and find her a good stick with a turn in the top that she could use as a cane.

On the first day he walked past many miles of farmland before he found a young sapling that was the perfect length and shape. But only he thought, it will not be strong enough to support her; "I have many more miles to travel, I am sure I will find a better one."

On the second day he found another stick, this one was much sturdier than the first, certainly strong enough to support her. But he worried that she would be disappointed with the knots in the wood and that surely a regal old gal like her would deserve a finer specimen; "I have many more miles to travel, I am sure I will find a better one."

On the third day he set off on his journey home, still thinking of what type of cane she would like. As he settled in to make his fire for the night, he found an aged piece of wood, just the perfect length, it also had a perfect curl for a handle, but he could see in the firelight, it was the color of old driftwood and he really began to wonder if it would last her all the rest of her days. In the morning he decided, "I have many more miles to travel, I am sure I will find a better one."

On his last day, the skies opened up and the rain
poured down on him. As her trudged through the
mud, he forgot about her cane; for a time that
is. Then, as the clouds started to clear, he found
himself close to home and back in the farmland,
nary a forest in sight, when he remembered...
"I can't go to her emptyhanded" he thought.
As he walked on, he came up to a lone apple
tree. Shrugging his shoulders, he set off
to cut her a branch suitable for a cane. The
branches, were short, gnarled and brittle.

As he arrived on her porch, his shoulders slumped,
apple branch in hand. He apologized to her, and
let her know that he had seen many more, better
sticks along his journey, but that he continued
on, expecting to find a better one for her.

"Young man", she said, This was like my life;
I met many, many fine men, but always
passed them over in search of a better one;
and that is why I am still an old maid.

Adapted from an oral story – Kaye Bryden

# Turtle Steps

SO FAST!
When young exuberance emerges.
SO STEADY...
When learning to go with the flow and ride the currents.
SO PRECISE...
When laying the nest of the future.
SO WISE!
Fulfilling, Enduring, Inspiring

PR

# AWAY...HOME?

As the sun rises over the water,
These tears
Fall from my face
As much as I love Cape Breton,
Now,
My home is in another place

My view
Is filled with forest
Big rigs, pipe underground.
Let me find the beauty in this flatland!
Great big sky,
And mud on the ground

As the sun shines over the water
Let me dry these tears from my face
As much as I miss the ocean
Now,
My home is in another place.

Well,
I moved to Alberta
Met a man that I adore
Have two children that I treasure
And,
On Cape Breton,
I close the door.

As the sun sets over the prairie
Now,
My dreams are coming all true!

Family,
Love,
And a Business...
What more can I Do?

PR

# Lifetime of Leaves

Like the cover of this book;
we are the tree...
Every person
who comes into our lives; the leaves
As a tree needs many, many leaves
to grow strong
Every individual needs connections
to thrive
Some leaves, nourish for awhile
then drop to the ground
Other leaves are large and strong and help
The branches reach for the sky....

PR

Printed in the United States
By Bookmasters